Amtrak Starbucks

Jazz on the Streets of Richmond

to the students poems

by John

Cover painting by John Peterson

copyright © 2018 John Peterson

ISBN: 978-0-9981469-9-7

Kvasir Books

An imprint of Poetic Matrix Press

www.poeticmatrix.com

Amtrak Starbucks

Jazz on the Streets of Richmond

Acknowlegments

Thanks to Devon for putting me up in Pink House for a couple
of years. And thanks to Cathrine for putting up with me.
Thanks to Joe Milosch for his critique and suggestions and to
Peter for his intoduction.

Also much thanks to the many Baristas for all the fine Lattes
everywhere.

And a special love to all the students who have grieved so
much.

Contents

Amtrak Starbucks
Jazz on the Streets of Richmond

To the Students

Introduction by Peter Friesen
Preface by Joe Milosch

Remember

Remember

Remember

Author Biography

To the Students

Introduction by Peter Friesen

If you are reading this, you are in for quite a treat, because these poems allow us to share something with a special person at an important time in his life

A little you should know about John. He has lived through some intense experiences. He drove a truck through the battle lines in Vietnam, and survived with his life and limbs intact. And returning home, he strayed from a pragmatic education, and studied philosophy, with much exposure to the eastern philosophical branches. All of it helped to cast him into the life of a poet, as a strategy, in a manner of speaking, of contending with things like beauty in the midst of ugliness. Along the way, he organized several outstanding restaurants, and raised two families.

He also founded a publishing company that gives a voice to poets of all kinds. He takes them under his wing, and sees the value in what they do.

John knows poetry better than most, and is one of its more accomplished craftsmen. What he has assembled here is a set of poems written in the aftermath of a divorce. I like this book so much that I am almost grateful for the divorce, because without it, I doubt we would have such a window into this gentle soul. Here there is pain, and joy, and something that straddles them, what John at times refers to as "beauty."

The poetry is disarmingly mature. He's not trying to impress the grownups because he knows he is one of them, and is in fact contending with being among the elderly—quite a shock to those of us who remember dressing in bandanas, discovering the legends of rock music, and marching against war. We were there celebrating youth, and now we are old. Oh well.

John doesn't beat around the bush. He starts right off, in his first work, entitled "Two Riding Amtrak," where he wonders ironically whether in his gaze at beauty he must "…like a beggar

…hide it from a prying world." (p. 17) But he's only just saying that, because in this book of poems he does quite the opposite.

And so, like the thinker that he is, he looks for ways to talk about beauty that accommodates what is complex and provocative about it. In one poem called "Darkness," he reaches for a foundation. "There are things that must hold together without effort. Things that need no saying, but are true. It is not possible to hold up without these." Even with that he writes: "I am not sure I can go further than the darkness." (p. 23) I can't really say why, but with that I couldn't suppress a smile.

He wasn't through with the subject of "Darkness" though. In another poem that he calls by the same title, he comes at it with a sledgehammer.

Do not lament in lack   nor seeking   you cannot find us
We are alive at your center   where it is warm   and full like

The night in a warm bed   legs entwined   finding secrets
For the 10,000th time   and always it is love that burst forth
bleeding (p. 30)

So much for "hiding it from a prying world."

It's not that John, or anyone else, is hiding something, but like he says in many different ways, it isn't the person who hides from beauty, but quite the other way around. Beauty must be uncovered, accessed, in an act of poetry. "It is not so hard to write, what is hard is to get the beauty down, because that is what is at the center, that must be found." (p. 41)

Beauty is not contained in generalized expressions. There is no meta-logic of beauty. It is, rather, onto-logic. It is part of a perfected image, existent in the moment of its expression. Go read "Keep this" on page 50.

The liquid amber is in trouble
All its leaves are every color
Gold like her skin
Like her hair
Running yellow gold like
Her   inside and out

At one level, we think: he misses his wife. But that is a superficial rendering. There is nothing quite as cool as one who marvels at the beauty of another, because in the process, they are showing you something about the experience of it. It is not a lament. It is a celebration.

But as John points out, sublime moments, the kind we think of as "beautiful" are lost in coarse environments, which is it seems, where John concludes. With several poetic statements about the resurgence of war culture, like our own, John calls us back to our younger halves, the ones that marched oh, say, 50 years ago. Many things of beauty came out of this vortex, in part, perhaps, we were able to be vigilant in opposing it—but not vigilant enough.

I think John is wondering if we have what it takes to stand against a world turned ugly, now for the umpteenth time. Can old men and women navigate such environments? I don't think I should say more to you without spoiling the ending. Go. Take it to Starbucks and read some of its gems aloud.

Peter Friesen, author of *On Freedom: Organizational Science Examined Philosophically*

Preface by Joe Milosch

I think a short piece of description of two locations in the poems would help center the poems and tie them to the title.

Amtrak

On stormy, winter days, I like riding the train along the coast to San Francisco. It is then that the rain and ocean odors invade the car. The passengers seem friendlier wearing their heavy shirts and light jackets. I listen to them share their story as they smile or I listen to music on my phone. The train seems friendly at these times. The lite white walls of the car are like a screen showing shadows of people like an Indian puppet show. In this atmosphere, I'm inspired to write.

Starbucks

During the summer, I visit Starbucks for my morning coffee. The high temperatures (100+) induce the people to hesitate before leaving to face the heat of the Central Valley. Outside, the nut and fruit trees line the roads and reflect the sunlight. I like sitting in the armchair and looking out across the farmland while I listen to the customers' friendly chatter.

It is at these times that the music from the Starbuck's sound system enchants me and I contemplate the beauty of community and music.

Joe Milosch, author of *Landscape of a Woman and a Hummingbird*

Remember

Two Riding Amtrak

Yes it is true
I cannot resist   to resist
Would be
An affront to nature   to god

So I must it seems   look your way
Gaze at you   through this prison
Your beauty   even
What lies at the heart   of your beauty

To voice it
Would be a pretense
So like a beggar I must hide it from
A prying world

I must it seems
Recognize you inside this glowing
Radiance that is your beauty
Like the velvet grass

Growing even now   between
The vines   down slope   from the pond
Hidden to everything
All around   everywhere.

You Are in the Air

You are in the air   from over there to here
You look unsure   but still you look

So we can at least say   yes   we had a meeting
Of sorts   I at least   can be thankful

It is these meetings that give satisfaction to the day
Whether long or short   there is something here

More than just   the passing of time
The meeting   of we two   on the long road

Today

If it had to happen it is good it happened here
This is cowboy town   bars and stock cars   but

You can sit in Starbucks and the jazz rhythms
Flow over you like San Francisco in fifty-nine

The latte is light
The jazz flows....

I said once that just maybe the taste of fine coffee
Might take the Revolution   a sip longer

How can you not feel more life when Ella sings out
A burning desire   under that old black magic   called love

Downtown Side

Today I chose the downtown side
Barbed wire   vacant lots   trash in places
Orchards yes and small houses

Tiny castles   dreams yes   love filled castles
Where the mystery is revealed nightly
Between sheets   between legs

So many mysteries   no one can seize them
They are safe   can never be taken by any
But the lovers   in that   we are sure

OK

OK   mid-morning on a Monday
With latte   hot and smooth
Diana Krall comin' through the speakers

Like the sun on my shoulders
It's Starbucks   coffee and sounds canned
From the hip board room   still   it's good

Traffic and Bart goin' by
The Richmond sun as fine here
As anywhere it shines

Perfect

Your every gesture
The wave of your hand
Touching your hair
Bending your head
Your wide-eyed expression

Each one perfect
How can this be
Every move   expression
Gesture   turn   exactly right
Full of grace and beauty

Your voice   your laugh
The angle of your leg
Your fine glassy skin
Your hair let down
Your fingers combing through it

You   full of grace and beauty
I now   full of grace   and beauty

Darkness

I am not sure I can go further than the darkness
It has been   my treasure and has saved what is faultless
But it does not hold well now

There are things that must hold together   without effort
Things that need no saying   but are true
It is not possible to hold up without these

And they go away over and over   and over again
What is left   is not the hollowed out silence
That measures what can be given   and received

I look around and there is beauty everywhere   but here
And it brings up what is so dangerous
That flood of dark water that turns and turns

I am not sure I can go further   than the darkness

Listen

If you listen
And don't know where it's going
That is ok

Everyone thinks they know
But then there is a turn
And they are amazed

But that is the way to see
Something that you have not seen

Dive Down

Go ahead   dive down
It is alright   something beautiful is there
You'll see

More beautiful then even you're sadness
It will take your sorrow and turn it
Cloudy and bright
Like the shine on that red amber place
You've seen once or twice

Just before everything was lost   or
Just before found

A gentle sax line on a street of the lost
Either waiting or consoling

Who can say

It can be a mood indigo
That will arrive again
At a perfect moment

When love is eternal
Is in all of us
Is in everything
Is one without second

Luminous

The fog is thick and a grey that is part
Luminous   and part opaque

It will cover us all   all the time   and as always
Turn into a moist   luminous   black

But this luminous grey is a hiding and we are pleased
Hiding is grateful sometimes   as there is a need

It comes from the same place and talks   in a still
Voice right to the second   and you are understanding

Regret gets to walk away into the fog-set once again
All is welling   there is no definition   and now walking

Sometimes obscured feet must plant in grey
It is the way of saints   and angel   of both castes

Sometimes angels sit and no one   doesn't know
But the fog and music blend in black and

We don't know   and say it is a sad elation that we do
Roads are long   and fogged in for a price   but we do

Sometimes

Sometimes in the obscurity   like
A sunrise behind a grey orchard
On an early   fog dripping   morning

You know there is nothing here
Ready to arise from the calming shroud
But still you cannot help   but die in wonder

Fear rises and rises
Your darkening eyes
A voice calling in fascination

The phantasm can arise from somewhere
And embody before your   eyes
Her beauty   draped in morning fog

The real and the unreal at the border
She   arising at that moment
Emerging   full blown   into your arms

This Emotion

Oh my this emotion   may be way more
It has not been before and now it is

It goes on for days   and yes for nights
You ride inside but it is all of loss and for something

Sade knows it but she can live it   I cannot
One time I had something   very pure and clear

Indeed I saw with clarity   what had happened to us
All that was missing was this   what we feel at the core

And now it is here and I am taken apart   and
Am lost   with us all

Morning

I sit in the cold wondering morning
My body of rare   form   like a wasted night
It has a need that is like a going bliss

If it could return we could be grateful
But it seems the ancient gods are off
Wandering empty paths   Gone resting

And I go with them if I can
If not I do not know   something
Is missing   and stays so

I've been here before   counting the many
Who travel   and I am amazed
I am but one of a multitude   who travel and travel

Until I come to the one of which I am   many
I could be loved or lost or maybe just a moment
But there have been times   just times

Darkness

Everything starts in darkness   the music is a cry from darkness
It is a pleading   a sorrow   a calling out   and we listen

We are not an absence of light   we are what light wishes to find
Wishes to marry and be complete

Do not lament in lack   nor in seeking   you cannot but find us
We are alive at your center   where it is warm   and full   like

The night in a warm bed   legs entwined   finding secrets
For the 10,000th time   and always it is love that burst forth
bleeding

When nothing is found   we are pure empty to the core
Nothing can fill us   nothing is us   nothing   no anything   we are

Amtrak

I ride Amtrak on a Saturday night
The folks are noisy here and there
The rail rhythms preach to the sound of voices

Seeing

I am seeing   almost   straining   and hearing too
More than ever   hearing you

Do you know what it is to hear someone   like morning
And see you   a streaming of particles against my face

What am I suppose to do   when you come   in such a way

No heard (heard somewhere)

When you first say a prayer you say by the mouth
Not from a book
Then you cut down a tree and make a book

I don't know what   about the tree

I Got it now

1

A triple shot and Miles at Starbucks

Gets it tastin' right
Oh   plus my heart in a breakin' mode

Coltrane low and sweet and then Miles
Playin' like he won't admit

A pretty blond pulls up on a Harley trike
Chewin' gum

Leather and fringe "Ride Free"
She been ridin' for so long   but she still got the look

All this mixed up   wrong year   wrong time
wrong heart   all broke up

Don't stay too far   don't stay too close
Stay just right   so you'll know

2

Oh yeah   Ella and Louie singin' "Porgy and Bess"
In the early morning with the espresso machine

In my solitude   with Billie   coming up next
I go mad with her Gladly   again and again

The folks steam in and out   a cup in the hand
Trying for that touch of mad   tinged with love

The sky is clear   the air warm   and I am a bit on the edge

3

Lookin' over the east bay from Richmond Point
San Francisco clear   I can see windows
And folks gazing out at the sky-writer sayin'

I don't know what

Flying down over The City   makin' a low run   a big loop
Crazy flyin' seven jets loopy low   Blue Angels maybe
Doin' a show for the folks   lookin' on

Jazz on the radio   piano riff like the riff over the golden bridge
Piano player and pilot givin' the folks a show
Feelin' it   low contrails for ears and eyes in the clarity of day

Feelin' good   Coltrane's sax   perfect as well
The Bay   perfect in the warmth of the day
I am   on such a day   in a good place   streamin' by

Void

Here it comes   a Rollin' of the void   you can hear it

Joy comes as well   see how it does that with a word

Singin' starts it   then music from her room
Then dancing   crazy like

Out of the darkness   out of the shadows showing her

If the tempo is right and the turning and the subtle mix

You can get a little crazy with her   you two together

But you wait   gone   taken away somewhere   you did not know

There it is maybe   just there ready to go   the dancing is ready

When it sweeps you   then the first

And there you are   gone in the night   a piece of light
vanishing into a warm patch of the fully dark

A last and beautiful look

That luminous   dark.

San Pablo Avenue

The streets are simple
San Pablo Avenue with many people   shops
And   cars   buses and Bart

It belong to you   It has your sound   your music
It holds you and makes your houses warm
Ready for   sex   love

I have seen so much of you
Beautiful women and girls men and boys
Making love   it is making love isn't it

We have so much power   we can make the most
Powerful   most beautiful thing in the universe

Indeed it is said that god is love and we
Together   make god   We make love

Here

I am here that is true
The music is different
And the people younger
More tattoos than once was

All of what I am is history
Slipped back from myself

I can show them once was
And form the future in a beat

And we go like rivulets of light
Chasing who we will be

Singin' that new song--they hear

The challenge is thus

Can we go more completely
Or have we gone as far as can be

If we have surveyed the whole   what now
Can we answer that question
Or are we dedicated to the endless pursuit
No matter the cost

But once we say   whole   it is now   one
And all goes on

Watershed

Is there a community of poetry
Or is that an error caused by presumption

Poetry is a piece of who makes a commune
Perfect combination of what is right

And what needs saying

Act

I write as an act of revelation   that is it you know
So I can see what is there to be seen
Because so much comes our way

So many impressions   so much impinges on us
So many ideas and constructs   all of these bodies
In motion   moving before us   it can be hard to keep up-right

And so I keep a language available   ready to reveal what is there
It is not so hard to write   what is hard
Is to get the beauty down
Because that is what is at the center   that must be found

Stockton graffiti "Can I Live?" seen from Amtrak.

Sadness

I do believe I have seen the saddest woman ever
So difficult to write   the sadness so great
That here   now as I write about this innocent encounter
I am stirred   dark water

She is maybe forty   six children
Her body rides low   heavy and harmed
Her face tired   with deep downward mouth   and
Sorrowful dark eyes

But it is from somewhere else where the well reaches
I apologize to her   that is all I can do   for the man who hurt her
For everything that hurt her   for god who did not find her
Pretty enough   to give her grace

Did not sustain her and show her that life
Is suppose to be beautiful
And joyful   and full of a universe you can trust

I can only apologize for all the sadness men cause women
All the sadness   god causes us all

Don't be afraid

Don't be afraid   let this in as deep as is its purpose
When the shape is matchless and god is in its purpose
It is beautiful and you are blessed   and we both are blessed

Gently see   gracefully engage   speak only of beauty
It is right you know to honor such beauty   to nod
And recognize without harm   with great appreciation

She enters and brings with her the perfect shape
She stands in its knowing   and full of grace and innocence
We are again blessed   all but beauty dismissed

She is real Of herself   Aphrodite's child
She is vindication that god is good in its purpose
We are blessed   the world renewed   and again
All is as it should be

Deep Place

Again that deep place   and again
Swung through a wind of you   a perfume filled
But with a sorrow of sadness

I am sorry for what we cause your beauty to show
What this incarnation has seen
and you are without

My tears   will join with you   and together   somewhere
We may forgive   this will not leave you
It is yours and mine now   it will

Stay   and together we will make it right again   and again
We are the strangeness that is us   together
And I am sorry

Give in

.

Wait   don't write that poem easily
Thrown most of what you write away

Wait like the fog rolling over that high valley wall
Arrayed in moon light   so silver   like her tears

Wait at the ocean shore until the sun is low
And the color of the cloud is just a searing hot scar

And the sea so dark you are unable   not
To go as deep   as deep as is not possible

Wait 'til beauty walks past you   and
You are stricken with shame that you did not know

Wait 'til that grieving child is rocked   and made whole
So many times

Wait 'til the hunger is dispersed to us all

Wait until we all   can actually breath easier
But the pain travels with us   still and will not allow

Wait and then wait again   until you have taken it all

Then

Starbucks

.

Well   I am taken by something unknowable
Beauty comes

From where   bursts
Into me and amazes me to my limits

I am pleased with just a look   a slight smile
And I so wish to sit   and talk and see

Who are you   this dark and unknowable person
I wish to speak with you   and for just a moment

Let our recognition   come in the fluttering
Noise of this place   that for now   because

Of your beauty   has become my high mountain temple
My great blessing in the midst

Billie

Billie's voice   playin' at Starbucks   in Escondido
It's perfect   really perfect   something   touching me just right

I remember reading a passage   in Steve Allen's
book   he at a party   when he heard of   Billie   passing

Goin'   into a closet   to find a darkening place
to be quiet with the gravity   of this space

I sat there darkly with him   for all these 59 years

Now I hear Billie's voice   and I am still   grateful
That I've heard what she   had to say

To me   over so   many   life times.

And occasionally   again   at Starbucks in Escondido
so many lives later   down the long long cooling road

36

36 years we sit and not a word
It is not the silence lost in a lover's gaze

It is not the monk in the mountain cave
It is just the sound of silence

I miss her

I missed her
And I miss her

I know first   that it is true
But sadness   I understand
As wildness leaves wreckage
Sweet and awful
Dreams collapse

The night is a portend
And a pointing finger

This verse is not of the past
Future springs from it
As it must from each moment

All that is different is what awakens
If she can hear
Is it different

 I wake to the same day

Keep this

They all keep this as it should be
Dark and light every day
Like it was   before we decided

The liquid amber is in trouble
All its leaves are every color
Gold like her skin
Like her hair
Running yellow gold like
Her   inside and out

It is a lot like confusion
So much beauty   in so many guises

It is the greater secret known to everyone
How can she hold such a secret
It is someone's amazement   given   without

The known and unknown
We are of this amazement
She has been hanging clothes
On a line   forever

When we don't see we can be grateful
When we see we are slain in that way
We are harmed   to our good

Couple

Couple in dark landscape.
Voices rise up from deep place   and speak
More voices rain down from a brilliant rich sky
The two speak in dance

Male moves to sky-place to converse

Female

People

People   if you knew the damage you do
With your sad   demeaning words

They have meaning you know   even in lies
They have pain   even in jest   but more so in failure

You can't run from them once released   they are
Your expression   and now your being

I do want to write of the high beauty
Where everything is in sweet perfection

It has been my joy to be there with you
But now   this day   I am in a place far down

Dark and warm with the speaker voice saying "come to me"
But I cannot   that is what fills this place

I can not

Catahoula

Now it's Catahoula and oh   the latte is fine
"Hey Jude" playing on a Saturday morning
At a distance we are all   so beautiful

As we come   get closer   the beauty can be exquisite
Even love and a perfect
Understanding   we can know who we are alone   together.

And yes it can be uncomfortable   we do not know   and then
Even after many years and love profound   something goes away
We do not know   what   or why

But forever after we will feel that fountain of sorrow
Rising over and over

In the light

In the light she arises   she fills this place
with beauty

Finally we are pleased   she glances my way
And I return   her look

We meet once again on this road
Of beauty and perfection

Coming

It has been coming for sometime
You just knew it like an orgasm building
And interrupted again and another time

Until you must go seek it
A treasure under a blanket of doubt
That must drain in

It is not always ecstatic   sometimes it is wrapped
In a dark voice waiting   and urgent
It sends a longing   sought forever

It is that way now   isn't it   there is disappointment
But a warm moist detachment   we would hold tightly
If we could   but   we cannot

It is madness that we are here again   only it is new
It never has been   it will wreak us   and we are fine
Wreak us again   for the first time   until

Beauty

     – Jack

There is beauty all around
There Is beauty all around

Whether near up or far back
There is beauty all around

If no one is here to see
There is beauty all around

If I am foolish and focused on this
There   was   beauty all around

There is beauty all around
There is beauty all around

So

So long and straight stretching the full length of you
So beautiful in your strength   and sound

Jazz on the street

Jazz on the street   flamencoSketches
Outside the Jazzschool on Addison
In the warm Berkeley day

It is right isn't it   jazz and poetry at the table
In the Kind of Blue day when Francisco
Lays back against a blue cover smiling

I've listened in the darkness   and that is good
And   next to a lady and   that is good
And now in the day as it wanes and the people stroll

It is good   and I feel the sway in hips and horn
And smile   and know that some hear these sounds
And know the source   as it swings   through horn   and hips

A thousand years

I can't find you but I want to find you
Like a thousand years ago when we met
On a high mountain meadow   the sun was low
And we again did not know where we were

We do not know now   and are in a whole
Battery of tears   we do not know   from
Whence they came   and yet here they are
Running like that damp rain pouring on us

It was before you were born   when I was wandering
And wandering still   you were coming   and no one knew
Certainly me but then you were there   and it was alright
Now you are again gone   unborn   again and I   want to find you

Blue In Green

These sounds are terrifying   I know them so well
Like the sounds I am made of   like he knew
Or made me wake like soft thunder in a near distance

Do we really need to go back   if something is left undone
Something in these notes   needs to waken us
Like we are not fully made   and he knew it would
Take more time

Here we go again   riding clear   into where they come from
I must follow again   and find
What we missed
There are many   frozen in pain for many lifetimes

Sung out of the dark   into a damaged world   still
We must find where we knew it would be   we'll try again
Again and again   until the pain is relieved

So many bodies

We are so many bodies you know   such that we
Show up   everywhere
There are so many of we you know   in so many places

What are we to do when each one is beautiful   like the first day
Exquisite like the night   just arriving

She calls out across a vast room   and   I remember
Somewhere in this noise   I've heard her voice   again

There are so many of we   so many and so beautiful   that I am
Overwhelmed   and really   happy to be a part   of this   we

We'll do this again   a few more times I'm sure
Just to check and see
If we did it right   or if we need to come back
Around again or again

Jazz and the Bay

Sunday morning warmth seeping in
A smooth piano and a done rhythm
Settles into places partly seen

They are the ones   some reason we can't tell
But the sax knows
It will be alright   someone says on a note
Somewhere   the bass will let us know

Something was and now so play
Whatever was amid   has a layer over
And climbs a guitar rif   with the day

Warmth cooks a bit but not beyond
It is ok   Lots of voices bring
And   sink and glide   and follow the breath of sax

Waiting

Waiting is what we do   a good part
We are that which waits
for the beginning of   next.

And is at best a mystery   and yet
we wait   sure it will fill us   and

Time

I can't go this much longer
That's all not much longer

There is This thing like a
Presence that envelops me

Like you   but you are a weight of tears
That were never spent

Now they are a sword and are aimed
What can become of this   nothing but a deepening

Scar with no end and no end
I'll last through it but there is no point now

It's just what is   but
Put some music to it   and I'll be alright

For now and the time coming

Us

There are so many of us   and we have but one prerogative
Take this as far as we can   right now.

If this is it   so be it   this is all that can be done   for now
On this swing around the sun   this is all there is to be

But the hints are so

Until

We speak of beauty and perfection but
they have meaning only   when

Feel is only a word   until

Real is only a word   until

The curve on the side of your breast
and our lips touch

Nothing is until

Beauty truth and love

We use them to recall   to take us again

You know   and we will again
It is alright   until

Remember

In the last hour

There is a sadness   spreading   over the land
I felt it before and I do not want it again

It is an ache   but more an overwhelming sadness

Returning from Vietnam   I felt something
But I was less able to feel   then
The times were different   I was different
But it was not good

And now it has invaded again

The children are hurt   pained   sad   others have gone crazy

My peers who went through it have again died   inside

We lost so many then   thousands/millions
Death does not forgive
It is lost when   purpose is fouled

It was fouled then   it is fouled now
And my peers will again pay deeply

We are betraying the young
As we were betrayed by our elders

We are fools and did not remember and now we betray
Them and they are filling with sadness   again

If   you deny them   you   you forget
That it is their world you leave
They will live in it and pass the pain you bequeath
On to their children

You betray them because of   your fear
Their was a war of our time   and like fools we give them
War / wars of their time   at home and in other's homes

We returned our brothers and sisters to the streets
To scream again that   they are in pain

Their peers are killing them

I remember many years ago feeling
That if we continue spreading pain
Around the world   eventually it will
Come back to us and hurt   us

We are hurt   but we blame those in pain
And sadness engulfs us

Remember the pain   is ours   we must own it
To shed it   we cannot shove it off to another
It is ours   we made it and now we must live it

Again   until our young teach us   again

There was a time   remember   remember
When we spoke   of something beautiful
We spoke to those in fear and   tried
To make it right   remember

That long long road became a burden
And we forgot   do not forget

Remember

We have gotten old   in our bodies as is our lot
But in our hearts   we have gotten   foolish

Remember   seeing that peace could finally
Come and gave him the prize   not for what he did
But for that peace that could   come   after 400 years

The prize   was peace

But again our fear was stoked   again we were betrayed
By our peers

And our sadness grows until it is choking us   choking us
And death will not   forgive
Not ever   until we remember   Remember

If you feel tears coming   let them flow
Until they cover again a great sob
For our young who tell us the truth
            again   again

Tell them you are sorry   tell them
They are the best of us

Don't betray them   you will die without
Understanding   you will die and leave
Nothing of value   you will leave only sadness

To the Students

To the students everywhere
You are heard

There are still old men that hear inside a sad Elation
You have the heart and we are there

What you do is deep   inside us all
Along the way

Care for all   the good   and the foolish
Take time to find joy   and love

Without it your heart breaks   find love and beauty
For all who have been lost   and harmed

That's the purpose in all this
You are love and you   love

The cycles come

We are not through yet
The age cycles
as simple as the day

But we are still in the early hour

As Siddhartha came to toil an
Hour for all time   our time is yet

As Jesus was the sun of an age and answered
Our age   on the precipice

The unveiling is still to come
And we are ready

The cycles come   small and large
No matter our desire

For James

Oh you have an immense Journey before you

You did what you did   you gifted us

Where you came from was deep and difficult

And you rose up beautiful
So Beautiful

And I am grateful for what you
Allowed me to see

It is all about beauty and you are

Beautiful

A Friend

To gather for a friend and help them
On their way   that is the final gift they give

They begin their   final coming and going
We celebrate their leaving and their

Flowing out along   a new journey

Remember

Boy of Art Girl of Poetry

The day is long in the barrel of the green world
Standing as it is in the corner of this place
Hidden from the carnage going on below

Like drawing back to the place of beginning
When the earth shot out pillars of beauty
Large planes of love and truth rode bareback

Art was a boy young and beautiful   Poetry was a girl
Full of desire and they ran screaming
Into the arms of each other without knowing
The order of things

Flashing about in the grass of a dizzy afternoon sun

Caught not as a thief but caught in the shadow
Steps of a thief behind the satisfied gaze
Of the neighborhood

Never caught by any but the thief

The clear forehead of innocence that would make
The body whole   the hard muscular night
That would purge the soul of aliens

The wandering look that would start small magical
Inhabitants squelling with delight
Because it was coming.

That rift   the tear in the membrane   the veil that
Was pulled over the eyes
And the heart by snarling old man beast

It was falling and nothing could stop it
Not the jealous rage of age or the wire wrapping
Of fear could stop it and the inhabitants of the old
World prepared to bathe and reignite

As the boy of art and the girl of poetry entered each other
The curtain fell about them golden Smelling of soft music
Small points of light danced up out of the abyss
To which they had been exiled

And the boy of art and the girl of poetry
Became their people and without form
Were scattered over the earth into the
Rock faces and tree spirits and into small bodies
Of animals   into the neighborhoods
Where old ladies cried themselves to sleep
Where old men wondered at their cruel deeds so long go

And the golden cord went out   wrapped itself
Around the mad girl on the ward

It went out to the children   without fathers

It went out without stopping

The boy of art and the girl of poetry could not
Stop the love that boiled between them

Though finally the world came between

Even so   late at night when the air is quiet
And the dog barks lowly in the distance   long
Tendrils leave their solar plexus
And travel the many dark miles   to join
Them together in some hidden place
Among the small inhabitants of hillsides
And stream banks.

And the tear is small   and the entrance reticent
But it goes on and it does not stop

And it goes on and on   and it is what love requires

Author Biography

John (Peterson) is the author of four previous books of poetry including: The Nature of Mountains; News of the Day; dark hills and wild mountains and Two Races One Face Two Faces One Race with Tomás Gayton. John along, with James Downs, is the publisher and editor of Poetic Matrix Press. As the publisher of Poetic Matrix Press, a literary small press, they have published more than 60 books of poetry and prose from writers across the country and around the world. In 2017 John, James and Joe Milosch edited and published Poetic Matrix Press Authors' 20th Anniversary Anthology 1997-2017 with cover art by Molly Weller.

John has read from his poetry, lectured and read at: the University of California San Diego; California State University San Diego; California State University Fresno; University for Humanistic Studies, Del Mar, CA; The Writing Center in San Diego; Palomar College San Marcos; Merced High School; Yosemite National Park including the Yosemite Centennial Celebration at the Ahwahnee Hotel in 1990; Ina Coolbirth Circle in Orinda; performances include venues in many communities.

Information on Poetic Matrix Press can be found at www.poeticmatrix.com